TEAMBUILDING

BULLET GUIDE

Mac Bride

Hodder Education, 338 Euston Road, London NW1 3BH

Hodder Education is an Hachette UK company

First published in UK 2011 by Hodder Education

This edition published 2011

www.hoddereducation.co.uk

Typeset by Stephen Rowling/Springworks

Printed in Spain

Contents

About the author

Mac Bride saw his first book published in 1982, and since then he has written more than 120 books on various aspects of programming, computer applications, the internet, language books for house buyers, green issues and other topics. When not writing, he typesets and oversees the production of books for several publishers, managing a scattered team of freelancers.

As a long-serving chair of governors, he has learned a great deal about building and managing teams of professionals and of volunteers.

Introduction

This book is not just for line managers in business. It's for anyone leading or involved in a team of any sort, whether it's a work group, a committee, a research team, a task force, a sports team, or whatever. All teams share certain characteristics and face some of the same challenges. What is crucial is **how the team is managed**.

A well-run team is greater than the sum of its parts – it can produce far more than its members could have produced individually. A badly run team is a bottomless pit down which its members pour their time and effort for little gain.

Teambuilding picks out the **key principles** and **practices** that enable a team to perform well. It will help leaders to develop, focus and motivate their teams, and it will help team members contribute more effectively.

1 Do you need to build a team?

What is a team?

A team has two essential components:

* a **common goal**
* a set of members who are **working together** towards that goal.

Without the common goal and the co-operation, it's just a group of individuals, each doing their own thing. A group of craftsmen or professionals, each working on their own project, is not a team, and trying to turn them into one would be a waste of time and energy.

Co-operation and a common goal turn a group into a team

The lifetime of a team is not an issue. A team may exist for as long as a casual game of football, for the duration of a project, or for many years.

A good team will achieve its goal, and its members will enjoy the process of getting there. But a good team rarely springs up fully formed; instead, it has to be built by conscious effort and **moulded into shape** by good leadership.

● There's more to being a team than just going in the same direction

What makes a high-performing team?

Whatever its size or function, and however long its lifespan, a team will perform best if it has certain features.

Within the team there need to be:

* a **shared purpose**
* **goals** that motivate
* clear individual **roles**
* good **communication**
* mutual **support**
* **diversity** of personalities, knowledge and talents
* **complementary skill sets**, with some overlaps.

● A high-performing team needs a shared purpose

Between the team and the wider world there need to be:

✳ enough practical **resources** to do the tasks
✳ good **communications**
✳ **support**, monitoring and motivation.

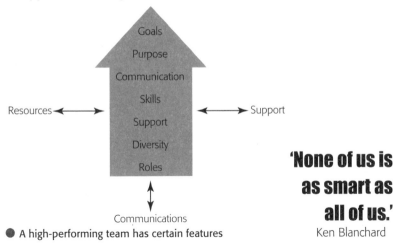

Resources ←——→

←——→ Support

Goals

Purpose

Communication

Skills

Support

Diversity

Roles

↕

Communications

● A high-performing team has certain features

**'None of us is
as smart as
all of us.'**
Ken Blanchard

Does 2 + 2 = 5?

The theory is:

'The whole is greater than the sum of its parts.'

The idea is that a cohesive group is more than the sum of its parts, and the output from a team is more than the total output would be if its members were working individually. The group as a whole outperforms even its best individual members working separately towards the same goal.

This is **synergy** at work. Team members encourage, support and challenge each other to greater effort, and they have the confidence and resources to do more than they would have managed alone. And it's not just about pooling different skills or combining strengths – it's also about **interactions** between members.

> Team members need individual **monitoring, motivation and management** if they are to give of their best.

Does 2 + 2 = 3?

On the other hand, this theory is not necessarily true. Total output may be lower because it's easier for people to slack off under cover of a team. The greater the size of the team, the more likely this is to occur.

CASE STUDY: Ringelmann's rope-pulling experiments

In the 1920s, Max Ringelmann, a German psychologist, found in rope-pulling experiments that three people exert only two and a half times the force of one person, and the difference increases as the group grows. Eight people exert only four times the force. Observation and analysis show that this is just as true today as it was in the last century.

The output from a team may be more – or less – than the total output of its members

Leaders and teams

Teams need leadership, but that doesn't mean that they have to have one person in charge. There are many different patterns.

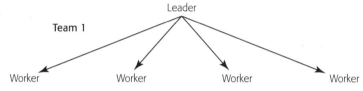

1 This is not a team. It's a gang of workers under a boss.

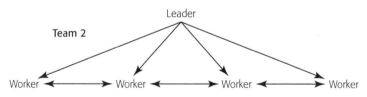

2 Here the workers may be forming into a team, but the boss is still separate.

8

3 This is more like a team – the leader and workers are all talking to each other, and communications are all two-way.

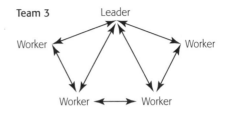

4 And here's a team where all members are equal. Leadership is shared, though one person may be given the role of co-ordinator.

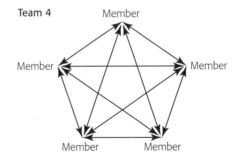

● Four types of team

How healthy is your team?

Run a health check on your team by asking yourself these questions:

☐ **Are the goals shared?**
  » If you ask all the members what the team's goals are, will they all give you the same answer?

☐ **Are the roles clearly understood?**
  » Does everyone know what's expected of them and how that contributes to the whole?

☐ **Do members see themselves as a team?**
  » Do they all know each other?

☐ **Are members all talking to each other?**
  » And just as important, are they listening?

☐ **Is the work getting done?**
  » Is it being done to time and of the required quality?

☐ **If someone is ill or away, do they leave a gap?**
  » Or can another member step in when needed?

☐ **Does the team have the resources it needs?**
  » This includes managerial support, as well as financing, equipment and other practical resources.
☐ **Does the team have efficient processes to solve problems and take decisions?**
  » This includes having effective team meetings, and being able to implement the most efficient ways of working.

1 If your answer is a definite 'yes' to all eight of these questions, you can probably stop reading now.
2 If you can answer 'yes' to some and 'no' to the rest, then there is work to be done, but at least you know your people.
3 If you don't know the answer to some of the questions, then you need to start talking with and listening to your team.

'Teamwork: simply stated, it is less me and more we.'

Anon.

2 Team development

How do teams develop?

Teams do not arise fully formed. They have to be built. In 1965 Bruce Tuckman, an American psychologist, proposed that, in order to grow and develop, teams must go through four stages:

* **forming** – getting to know each other and getting organized
* **storming** – trying to resolve conflicting ideas
* **norming** – working to agreed goals and methods
* **performing** – delivering extra value through close teamwork.

Teams do not arise fully formed. They have to be built

Not all teams reach the performing stage; some never get past storming.

In 1977 Tuckman added a fifth stage, *adjourning*, for when the task is done and the team is disbanded. As this book is about **building** teams, we'll ignore that stage.

There is no timescale here; any stage can last any length of time. Progress can stop at any stage, and teams can revert to earlier stages, for example if their membership changes.

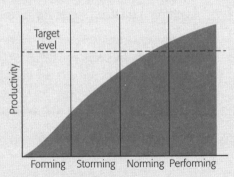

● Stages in team development

Forming

In the **forming** stage, people are trying to:

* get to know one another
* understand the team's objectives.

People are usually on their best behaviour, preferring to establish relationships before they tackle any difficult issues. The focus is on **getting organized,** agreeing goals and allocating tasks.

Not much actual work will be done at this stage, while you are putting the essential **framework** into place. Good leadership is always crucial, but during this first phase you will need to be quite directive. You must ensure that all the team members know the team's goals and their own and everyone else's roles, and when, where and why the team will be meeting.

'There is no "I" in "Team".'

Anon.

16

Tips for faster forming

1 Have the essential **resources**, such as workspaces, equipment and finance, in place at the start.

2 Use **icebreakers** to help people get to know one another (see chapter 9).

3 Be clear yourself about the team's **goals** and make sure that your team knows them very early on (see chapter 5).

4 Encourage **informal activities** for members – even a common coffee area will help.

> People are still working largely as individuals at this stage. Take the opportunity to assess each member's strengths.

● At the forming stage leaders need to be quite directive

Storming

The **storming** stage is marked by conflict and – if the team is to be successful – by resolution. The conflicts are about:

* **identifying the problems** to be solved
* deciding how the group is to be **organized** and led
* working out how members will work **by themselves and as a team**.

This stage can be very productive if members are tolerant of each other and discuss ideas freely, keeping the focus on the real issues and the team's **overriding goals**. If personalities get in the way of **co-operation**, or discussions get bogged down in minor details, the team may not move beyond the storming stage.

> A key task of the leader here is to guide the debates so that members can participate freely and resolve their differences smoothly.

Tips for smoother storming

1 Discuss the forming–storming–norming–performing concept with the team. Knowing what you are going through and what lies ahead can help you get there.

2 Run team **meetings** productively (see chapter 6).

3 Set individual and group **incentives** that reward co-operation (see chapter 8).

4 Encourage better interpersonal **relationships** through non-work activities.

5 Identify reluctant/uncommitted/ uncertain members. Talk through their **problems** and try to resolve them.

6 If necessary, neutralize any disruptive members (see chapter 8).

● The storming stage

Norming

In sociology jargon, a norm is an accepted way of behaving or doing things within a group. If it reaches the **norming** stage, a team has:

* evolved its own rules and sense of being a group
* a single agreed goal (or set of goals) that all members are working towards co-operatively.

Although there may be **debates** about means, they are open and positive, not disruptive. People know their roles and their place in the team. Energies can now be focused on doing the work.

People know their place in the team

Leaders delegate tasks and oversee progress but they no longer need to instruct. They may have an important role in assisting the personal development of team members.

From norming back to storming

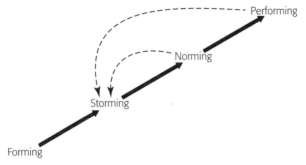

Performing

Norming

Storming

Forming

● **The norming back to storming cycle**

The basic route is upwards, but the path may not be direct. A team may come back from the norming (or even performing) stage to **storming** if its goals, membership or other key factors change. The cycle may be repeated many times over the life of the team.

Each new phase of storming should be easier to resolve than the last, since the team is now used to working co-operatively.

Performing

The **performing** team is a high-performing team. At this stage the team:

* is clear about its goals and strategies
* can act independently and take its own decisions, within terms and to criteria agreed with its leader.

Its structures and processes fully support the team's performance. The team can diagnose and **solve its problems**, and implement the necessary changes. As it is now channelling all its energy into the tasks, it achieves its goals and strives to exceed them.

> Leadership is now mainly about facilitating and motivating. Some aspects of leadership will have been delegated to or assumed by team members.

'Teamwork is the fuel that allows common people to attain uncommon results.'

Anon.

From norming to performing

The two qualities your team needs to be able to take the step from **norming** to **performing** are:

* confidence
  * » There's nothing like knowing you can succeed to enable you to do things. A team's confidence will grow over time but it could be given a boost through an achievement-based team game. Show people what they can achieve as a team, and that self-belief will carry over into their work.
* motivation
  * » The prospect of a job well done – especially as part of a team – is a great motivator, but financial or other incentives rarely go amiss.

> **Find out more**
> See also chapter 8 on motivation and chapters 9 and 10 on teambuilding games.

3 Who's on your team?

What does your team need?

Unless you are forming a relay team, where all you want is speed, you will normally need a range of **skills, qualities and personalities** on your team. In part this is to meet the requirements of the task – whatever that may be – and in part because teams thrive on **diversity**.

You must keep the need for diversity in mind when:

* recruiting a team from scratch
* expanding the team or replacing a member.

People contribute in different ways in different situations

'Diversity without unity makes about as much sense as dishing up flour, sugar, water, eggs, shortening and baking powder on a plate and calling it a cake.'

C. William Pollard

People contribute in different ways in different situations. A team may have all the **technical skills** needed to handle its task but, if none of its members have the personal qualities and **interpersonal skills** to form good relationships, it will not become an effective team.

You might look at diversity in terms of:

* skills
* personality
* culture
* starters and finishers.

The range of skills

What range or, rather, ranges of skills does the team require?

Skills can be grouped into three broad categories:

* **technical** – in the broad sense of knowing how to do things, from the skilled salesman who knows how to pitch to a difficult market to the engineer who can calculate the stresses on a cantilever bridge
* **problem solving** – able to make the creative leaps that produce new answers to new (and old) problems. And if someone has both problem-solving and technical skills, there is even a decent chance that the answers might work first time!
* **interpersonal** – able to command, communicate, co-operate, cajole and/or otherwise interact effectively with other people.

People often have skills in more than one category. What matters is the total of the skills available in the team as a whole.

What skills does your team need?

When assembling a team, start by working out the skills it will need to achieve its aim. It doesn't matter whether the aim is to win football matches, break into a new sales market or build a pipeline through Siberia.

You can analyse any result in terms of the **components** or stages that combine to produce it, and the **skills** needed at all levels. The more you break down tasks into sub-tasks, the better you will identify the skills you need.

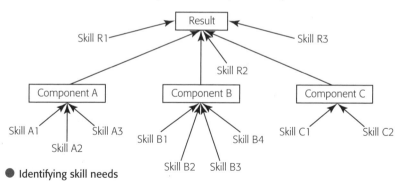

● Identifying skill needs

Starters and finishers...

Every project needs its starters and its finishers.

Starters

These are ideas people. They love to come up with new ideas and solutions to problems, but their excitement and interest are in that initial creation. They are not so strong on attention to detail or the consistent application needed to get the job done.

Finishers

These are those more organized people who see a job through to the end. They draw everything together, test and check and redo until the product is right. Finishers are typically quieter, less flamboyant people than starters but they must not be overlooked.

'Without starters, the project will never get off the ground. Without finishers it will never fly.'

Sam Kennington

...and other types

Other types of people can also be useful to have around.

* **Simplifiers** can make a real difference if brought in before
  implementation starts. They will pare a project down to its essentials,
  and add trimmings back in only if they will add value.
* **Detailers** can help to ensure that things are done
  properly. Attention to detail is a key ingredient of
  success.

However, there are some types you can do without:

* **Critics** find fault and undermine morale.
  Constructive criticism is good; carping is
  destructive.
* **Tinkerers** keep fiddling with things, which may
  or may not make them better, but will certainly
  delay completion.
* **Procrastinators** are not to be tolerated.

● 'Someone has to
look at the details...'

Diversity is strength

You might think that a team consisting only of dynamic young men educated in the best schools and universities would be a sure-fire winner. And it could be – for a rowing eight or, possibly, a rugby team. In almost every other situation such a team would fail to achieve its potential, especially in marketing, customer service or the public sector.

The lack of diversity would mean that:

* all members would approach problems from much the same angle
* at best, the team would lack fresh ideas
* at worst, the team would fall into the trap of **'groupthink'**, where it can envisage only one possible answer – which may well be completely wrong.

'You don't get harmony when everybody sings the same note.'
Doug Floyd

What sort of diversity?

You want as many sorts as possible, but the crucial ones are:

* **gender** – men and women tend to think differently
* **age** – balance experience against freshness
* **culture** – this affects attitudes, beliefs, education and many other aspects of life.

A diverse team will have a range of viewpoints, and can potentially offer a greater variety of solutions to problems.

Diversity and the law
It's against the law to discriminate against employees on the grounds of race, gender, age or disability, but given the benefits of diversity, why would any sensible organization want to do so anyway?

Without diversity, all team members will tend to approach problems from the same angle

Unity from diversity

Every team needs to agree **ground rules** for how it works together, and these should arise from the team members' shared values. Ground rules govern such things as:

* how and when the team meets
* how members interact in meetings and in their daily work
* how the team interacts with the wider organization.

External factors may determine the rules, but the team can decide how to interpret and implement them.

Establishing the rules over several sessions will give members a better understanding of one another's values.

Even a team consisting of 'the same sort of people' may contain hidden differences in core values. Failure to explore these and to build from them can lead to conflict and misunderstanding later.

Setting ground rules

1 Ask each member to note down five things that they value most in the workplace.
   » These may be specific or vague: for example, clarity in communications, meeting deadlines, honesty, respect.

2 **Share the values.**
   » Write them on a whiteboard, flip chart or large sheet of paper.

3 **Discuss them as a group.**
   » Allow all the team members to give their opinion.
   » Then identify one value that all can agree on.

4 **Formulate a rule from the value.**
   » Translate broader values, like 'respect', into specific actions such as 'listening without interruption in meetings' or 'not expecting others to wash up your coffee mug'.

● The values might be vague…

4 Leadership

What makes a good leader?

Good leadership is an essential component of a successful team. Very few people are natural leaders, but leadership skills and techniques can be learned.

The leader serves a number of functions, and the qualities required can vary in different situations, but the key generic ones revolve around the **vision**. The good leader:

* has a clear vision of the future
* communicates the vision to the team
* gets people to commit to the vision.

Good leadership is an essential component of a successful team

....

> **'Vision is the art of seeing the invisible.'**
> Jonathan Swift

The vision and the team's commitment to it are the start. To be able to build an effective team to implement the vision, the leader must inspire **loyalty** by earning:

* **respect** – the leader must have the qualities and skills to deliver
* **trust** – the team must know that the leader will look after their interests.

● Leaders must get their teams to buy into their vision

Tips for being a better leader

Take each point and think how you could translate it into practice with your team.

1 Articulate your vision	Team members need to know where they are going and how they can contribute.
2 Define success	Your team must understand what success looks like, so that they recognize it when they get there.
3 Set incentives for the group…	These are to be shared by the group and are to depend on the group's effort.
4 …not individual rewards	Competition between members reduces co-operation.
5 Take responsibility for failures…	If a team member fails, the leader should take any blame coming from outside.
6 …but share success	When the team succeeds, make clear that it is their success, not yours.

7 Have clear accountability	Who is responsible for what, and to whom do they report?
8 Delegate tasks carefully	Make sure that the person knows what to do and how to do it (see later in this chapter).
9 Delegate decision-making power	Empowering the team will help boost their growth and achievement.
10 Be truthful, and ask for the truth	If you mislead the team, they won't strive for you. If they don't tell you about problems early on, you'll have bigger problems later.
11 Deal with conflicts swiftly	Intervene as soon as you realize that people are not getting on.
12 Encourage personal growth	Offer professional development opportunities to your staff.

Finally, make sure the team has the **resources** it needs.

Actions and styles

What team members need from their leader will change as the team goes through different stages of development.

Forming: set the goals

The essence of the leader's job at this stage is to get the team together and set up a basic **structure**.

* Set the overall objectives for the team.
* Allocate tasks and roles to individuals.
* Get communication going with your team members and within the team.
* Be directive and tell people what to do.

● Set the objectives for the team

42

Storming: resolve conflicts

As people get more involved in the project, there will be disagreements, mainly about ways and means. The leader's job is to turn these into **positive discussions** that take the group forward.

* Resolve conflict, seeking consensus and fresh ideas.
* Encourage interaction between individuals.
* Foster co-operation on tasks and team bonding.
* Be largely directive, but consult team members and draw on their growing expertise.

Does size matter?
The most effective teams seem to be those of between four and 12 members. With fewer than four, a team may lack sufficient diversity of thought and/or the required range of skills. With more than 12, it becomes difficult to achieve a high level of group cohesion.

Norming: facilitate

By now, the individuals have become a functioning team and you can switch the emphasis to getting the job done.

* Ensure that the team has the **resources** it needs.
* **Co-ordinate** work on different aspects of the job.
* **Facilitate** the team's processes.
* **Listen to and advise**, rather than direct, team members.

A confident leader does not try to micro-manage the team but still stays close to the team through regular meetings. Make it clear that, if team members need advice or assistance, you are always there to facilitate and support.

'No one can whistle a symphony. It takes an orchestra to play it.'

H. E. Luccock

Performing: empower

Once a team is fully formed to the performing level, the best thing a leader can do is let it get on with things without interference. You can **support your staff** best by believing in them and letting them know that you trust them to solve most problems by themselves.

* **Mentor** and coach as needed.
* **Encourage** the team's self-development.
* **Empower** the team to make its own decisions.
* **Step back** and watch, providing support where needed.

Support your staff by believing in them

● Teams need regular nurturing

The art of delegation

To be successful at delegating tasks and responsibilities to individuals or to teams, you need to **plan** carefully. The person or group who will take on the task must have:

* the ability to do the job
* the skills that the job needs
* a clear understanding of what is required.

If any one of these elements is missing, things may well go wrong. It's up to you to ensure that the skills and understanding are in place.

> **Remember**
> Failure does nothing for team development, but success empowers teams.

'Don't tell people how to do things. Tell them what to do and let them surprise you with their results.'

General George S. Patton

Training for delegating

There are broadly three types of delegation you can use, depending on the job and the level of experience of the team member.

Type 1: hand holding

You are with the trainee all the way through the process.

Type 2: checkpoints

You check and correct progress at key points. These are small inputs of time but they can interrupt other workflow.

Type 3: full delegation

You hand the job over at the start and collect it at the end – a major time saving.

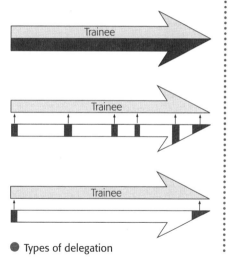

● Types of delegation

5 Goal!

The team's goals

There are four steps to consider when you think about your team's goals:

1 setting the goals
2 getting the team to buy into them
3 working out how to achieve them
4 achieving them.

Although there may appear to be only one simple goal, we talk about goals in the plural because, when you look more closely, it will almost certainly break down into several **components or sub-goals** and/or a number of stages.

People will strive their hardest to reach the team's goal if they feel that it is also their personal goal.

People will strive hardest to reach the team's goal if they feel it is *their* goal

● Without clearly understood goals, teams will achieve little

Goals and teams

At the very least, a team will have two fundamental sets of goals.

Goals for the team

These will normally be **set by exterior forces**, which could be:

* higher management
* business pressures
* government policy.

There will be one or more main goals, and often some subordinate goals that feed into them. Here are two examples.

* A football team manager might set his players the modest goal 'to avoid further relegation', or aim high with 'win the cup, get promotion and beat two arch rivals on the way'.
* A customer service team may be tasked with achieving 95 per cent customer satisfaction scores, and part of this may be to keep on-hold times to under three minutes, and completion time to under ten minutes.

The team is the goal

To achieve its goals, the team will need to reach a high level of effectiveness. This means that becoming a **high-functioning team** is in itself a goal, and reaching the storming and norming stages are goals along the way.

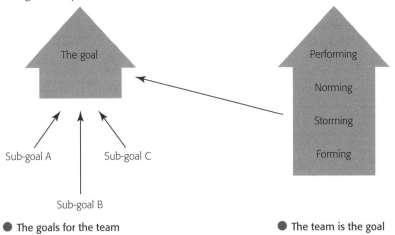

● The goals for the team

● The team is the goal

Defining the goals

People need to feel that the team's goal is their goal. But how can team members gain **ownership** of the goal if it has been set from outside? Here's one way. It may not produce full ownership of the ultimate goal, but it will give ownership of the sub-goals, which directly relate to actions.

The process needs to start at the first team meeting, and be picked up again at later meetings.

1 Lay out the team's overall goal. It can be quite vague: 'increase profits', 'provide a better service' or 'build a world-beating widget'.
2 Explain why you need to reach the goal. The reason might be 'because the public needs a better service' or 'because we'll all be out of a job otherwise'.

'When it is obvious that the goals cannot be reached by your actions, don't adjust the goals, adjust the actions.'

Confucius

3 Work with the team to define the goal in terms of measurable outcomes. All team members must contribute to the definition, which might be, for example, 'increase profits by ten per cent in six months' or 'cut queuing times by half by November'.

4 Break down the overall goal into the sub-goals that feed into it, as shown in the table.

Overall goal: increase profits by 10%				
Sub goal: increase profits		Sub-goal: cut costs		
Find new markets	Improve margins	Cut production costs	Cut staff costs	Make efficiency savings

a **Define** the sub-goals, and break them down further until you have ones that can be reached by specific actions.

b **Prioritize** the actions, and set the team to work!

SMART goals

Use the **SMART** approach to set your goals, and you will have a more realistic chance of achieving them. The SMART mnemonic means:

☐ **S**pecific
  » This means clearly defined. 'Sell more stuff' is not specific. 'Sell ten per cent more standard widgets and 50,000 of the new improved widget' is.

☐ **M**easurable
  » This means deciding how you will know when you have reached your goal. Will you have a physical object or a chunk of money in the bank?

☐ **A**chievable
  » Is it within your capabilities, and do you have the time and other resources that you need?

☐ **R**ewarding
  » In what way will you be better off for doing it?

☐ **T**ime-based
  » When must it be done by?

From goals to tasks

As goals are broken down into sub-goals, it becomes easier to see what's needed to achieve them. At the lowest level, **a SMART goal defines a task**. For example:

1 The top-level goal is 'Sell 50,000 new widgets this year, making £100,000 profit'. This is SMART, but raises a host of 'how?' questions.
2 Several levels down you might find the goal 'Have 10,000 brochures ready by 1 June'.
3 This can be further broken down into goals for the production of text, images and design, and arrangements for printing. Those can be translated directly into tasks allocated to individuals.

SMART goals are worthless if they are not accepted by those responsible for them. Top-level goals must be agreed by the whole team, lower-level ones by individual members.

Knowing your place

All goals should arise from the team's main goal, but you should never lose sight of that main goal.

1 **Talk to your team members** one by one, and ask them what they see as their goal.
2 **Prompt them** – if necessary – to tell you how this relates to the team's goal.
3 **Repeat the process** for all members.
4 If only one or two members cannot give a clear response, they may be non-players. You need to work on getting them to **sign up** to the team or moving them out of it (see chapter 8).
5 If a significant number cannot relate their work to the team's work, you need to look again at your **goal-setting processes**.

Never lose sight of the team's main goal

Do this exercise during **casual conversations** rather than at formal performance reviews. You need to know how far the goals have become part of people's normal working life.

CASE STUDY: The Williams Formula One motor racing team

The team's goal was 'to make the cars go faster', and everyone in the workshop said how their work contributed to this. For instance, 'I'm designing an aerofoil. If I get it right, it'll make the cars go faster.' When the tea lady was asked what she did, she replied: 'I just make the tea and hand out cookies.' She then added, 'So that these lovely boys can make the cars go faster.'

(Scot McKee, *Creative B2B Branding (no, really)*)

6 Meetings

Why have meetings?

Meetings must have a real purpose or else they are a waste of time. Whether your meetings are daily, weekly or monthly – which will depend on your type of work – keep them **short, focused and action-orientated**.

Whatever the prime purpose of a meeting, things will be happening beneath the surface. Positive interactions will be reinforcing the team's sense of identity, while negative interactions will be pushing the members apart.

> **'Coming together is a beginning.**
> **Keeping together is progress.**
> **Working together is success.'**
> Henry Ford

The team may meet in different combinations, for different reasons.

* **Whole team meetings** are for sharing information and making decisions on overall goals, strategies and outcomes.
* **Sub-group meetings** are for detailed planning of specific aspects of the team's work.
* **One-to-one meetings** are a chance for you to 'catch up' with individual progress; they may be formal or informal.

● One-to-ones may be informal…

The team may meet in different combinations, for different reasons

Meetings with purpose

Valid reasons for holding a meeting are to:

✔ *update people on progress*
✔ *share information and ideas*
✔ *decide what to do next*
✔ *allocate tasks and responsibilities*
✔ *reinforce group identity.*

The best meetings generate new and exciting **ideas**, and allow everyone to have a say before allocating the resulting **tasks** and **responsibilities** among the individual team members. To encourage people to put forward **suggestions** or express a view, try saying something like 'I'd be interested to know what Paul thinks', or 'I think Amy would like to make a point.'

Top tip
If the only purpose of a meeting is to reinforce group identity, then a social activity is probably more effective than a meeting.

The following are *not* valid reasons for holding a meeting:

✗ *'We always have one on Tuesdays.'*
✗ *'People like us are supposed to have meetings.'*
✗ *'We need to arrange a meeting.'*

> If information is being given out without discussion, meetings are rarely the most efficient way to do this.

Go to a meeting only if you can answer yes to at least one of these questions:

☐ Do I have something to contribute?
☐ Will I gain something from it?

If all you are doing is observing, you shouldn't be there. Keep abreast of what's going on by reading the **minutes**.

'Meetings are indispensable when you don't want to do anything.'

J. K. Galbraith

● 'This meeting is pointless...'

Making better use of meetings

Make the best use of meetings, and encourage the other participants to do the same.

Be prepared

1 If you are in charge of the meeting, create an **agenda** and get it out to the participants in good time.
2 Don't put 'Any other business' on the agenda. If people want to raise matters, they should let you know in advance.
3 If there are documents to be discussed, circulate them beforehand.
4 Read the agenda, the minutes of the last meeting and any documents before you go.
5 Make a note of any points you want to raise.
6 Be there on time. And if you are in charge, start on time.

● Always start on time!

66

Stick to the agenda

If you are running the meeting:

* agree an end time before you start, and keep to it
* if it's a full agenda, set time limits for items
* keep the meeting to the agenda
* encourage participation, but make sure people stick to the point.

If you are not running the meeting, try to encourage whoever is to follow these rules.

If it's a full agenda, set time limits for items

Good minutes

Good minutes can save hours. Good minutes are:

* **short:** they record decisions made, with summaries of discussions if relevant
* **action-based:** they say what needs to be done and by whom
* **promptly produced:** they go out soon after the meeting.

Six thinking hats

The 'six thinking hats' technique is based on the concept that there are six different types of thinking. These are associated with colours.

* **White is about information** – listing or seeking out the facts of the matter.
* **Red is for emotions** – likes and fears, and the gut reaction to ideas.
* **Black is for critical judgement** – looking for problems or flaws in the plan.
* **Yellow is for positive thought** – looking for benefits and taking an optimistic view of potential outcomes.
* **Green is creative** – the green shoots of fresh ideas, following up lines of thought into new areas.
* **Blue is the controller** – it oversees the thinking process.

The technique can improve the effectiveness of group discussions and individual thought processes. If all types of thought are brought to bear on a problem, you are more likely to reach a better **solution**.

Individually, you can apply the approach by donning the metaphorical hats as you look at a situation from different angles. In a group situation, actual hats can be useful to ensure that at least one member is adopting each mode.

The technique was popularized by Edward de Bono in his book *Six Thinking Hats*, but the original idea is claimed by Michael Hewitt-Gleeson of the School of Thinking. Wikipedia is a good place to start finding out more about the technique and its origins.

Six thinking hats: parallel thinking

In a group situation, the six hats technique should be used with '**parallel thinking**'. The essence of this is that people concentrate their energies on their own thoughts, rather than attacking the ideas of others. This can be managed in several ways, as shown in the table opposite.

The leader needs to keep the blue hat on – or close at hand – at all times, to bring people back into the appropriate way of thinking, if they stray.

It's not personal
This technique is a good way of dealing with people whose contributions are unhelpful. Instead of criticizing a hopeless optimist, you can compliment them on their yellow hat thinking, and then ask them to try the black hat.

Six thinking hats in practice

All together now!	Think differently	Pass the hat
All members of the team wear the same colour hat, so they are all thinking the same way. What they put forward should tend to reinforce or **add breadth** to the ideas of others. If everyone goes black, problems will be explored; with everyone yellow, a fuller picture of possible benefits will be seen.	People wear hats that go against their natural inclination or current position on an issue. As a way of getting people to **see another side** of a situation, this can be more effective than argument.	Circulate the hats round the group, passing them on as ideas dry up. This gets everyone to approach the problem from different angles, but bringing **new ideas** into the group with each change of hats.

'If you wait for opportunities to occur, you will be one of the crowd.'

Edward de Bono

7 Communications

Communicate!

Good communications lie at the heart of every successful team. People need to be able to speak freely with each other and to share ideas, good news and bad news.

Sometimes you, as the leader of your team, will just want to get your **message** across loud and clear, but most of the time communications within a team should be **two-way**, so that everyone in the team feels heard and understood.

Good communications lie at the heart of every successful team

'In teamwork, silence isn't golden, it's deadly.'

Mark Sanborn

Communications can be at several levels. All have an important part to play.

* **Noticeboards** are good for announcements, especially of social events.
* **Email** is ideal for one-to-one conversations or file sharing.
* **Group emails** are suitable for information sharing.
* **Chats** around the coffee machine can be good for bouncing ideas around, as well as for social bonding.

● There are many ways to communicate

Better listening

Communication is a two-way process. Listening is a crucial part of it – and there's more to it than just hearing. It's about fully taking in the other person's message.

1 Try to get the environment right.	Choose a quiet place and/or switch off distractions if possible. You need to be able to hear. People will speak more easily if they don't have to shout.
2 Give them your full attention.	Stop whatever you are doing and don't fiddle with things. They need to see that you are really listening.
3 Look at the speaker.	It shows them that you are listening, and so encourages them to talk. It also enables you to pick up non-verbal clues from their facial expressions and body language.
4 Don't interrupt.	And don't jump in as soon as they pause; they may need a moment to work out how to say the next bit.

5 Don't think about your reply.	Give your mind over to listening. Wait until they have finished, then think over what has been said before you decide how to reply.
6 Give them feedback.	Nod, smile or make a sympathetic noise, to show that you are listening and to encourage them to go on.
7 Get clarification.	Ask questions when you do not understand. If you are not sure about a point, paraphrase it back to them to check that you have understood it.
8 Try to look beneath the surface.	Are there other issues beneath what is being said? Look for non-verbal clues, and consider the context in which this person works.

'Nature gave us one tongue and two ears so we could hear twice as much as we speak.'

Epictetus

Email: informing not overloading

Used properly, email can really help to knit a group together, no matter how physically far apart its members may be. Email is **convenient** to use and saves time, as long as people read only the messages they need to, and don't get bogged down in others.

Use email for:

✔ *group mailings, to spread information, call meetings or ask for help*
✔ *sharing ideas informally with one or more members*
✔ *reporting progress or problems*
✔ *circulating documents and other files.*

Group mailings
The team leader (and others, if appropriate) should have all the team's addresses in a mail group, so that a single message can be sent to everyone easily.

Six good practice tips for emailing

1 Only send messages to the team members who need them, or who have asked to be copied in to email exchanges. Overuse of cc or 'reply all' wastes time.

2 Always fill in the **subject line** with a clear description of the purpose of the message. It will enable recipients to decide its importance, and it will simplify their filing later.

3 Don't reply to an email just to acknowledge receipt, unless there have been past problems with the email, or you need to for legal reasons.

4 **KISS** – Keep It Short and Simple.

5 **Spellcheck** your messages, then reread them before sending to be sure that your message is clear.

6 To ensure that your emails don't seem demanding or terse, always include a **courteous** greeting and closing.

Email can really help to knit a group together

Scattered teams

Not all teams are based in the same office, the same building or even the same country. In a national or a global business, a team's members may be scattered across half a dozen or more offices and rarely, if ever, meet together. Such a team may consist of:

* people with different skills, working on a joint project, who need to keep abreast of each other's progress
* managers or practitioners in equivalent posts in separate offices who need to co-ordinate their work and share information and good practice.

Whatever the nature of the team, good communications are essential to overcome the barriers of distance. You'll need to create **clear rules** and **expectations** that everyone understands.

● Spell out your meaning in detail

Six tips for better communications in scattered teams

1 **Meet regularly** – via conference calls or online meeting rooms – and aim for maximum attendance every time.

2 **Encourage informal online meetings** – you can't gather round the water cooler or teapot but you can chat through Skype or Messenger.

3 **Give team emails priority.** All members should read and reply to emails from other members before dealing with mail from outside.

4 **Explain things fully** – when communication is not face to face, there are no non-verbal clues, so spell out your meaning in detail.

5 **Have a central document store** so that everyone has easy access to the team's data.

6 **Don't forget time differences** – schedule contacts to suit people's time zones and office hours.

'The single biggest problem in communication is the illusion that it has taken place.'

George Bernard Shaw

Virtual meetings

Modern telecoms and web technology enable virtual meetings to be held easily and at little or no cost. **Conference calls** can be accessed by anyone with a phone or a PC, and **video conferencing** through the web is feasible if everyone in the team has fast broadband access.

The advantages

Compared with face-to-face meetings, virtual meetings are:

* **cheaper** – there are no travel or accommodation costs
* **more time-efficient** – no time is wasted in travelling
* **easier to arrange at short notice** – people only have to find a slot for the meeting itself and not for also getting there and back
* **more flexible** – members or outside consultants can 'attend' just for the part relevant to them.

The disadvantages

There are two distinct disadvantages.

* Virtual meetings need **more directed chairing** to keep discussions on track and ensure that everyone gets a hearing.
* Participants may not stay focused and may be tempted to try to **multitask**, e.g. check emails or put the final touches to a report, during an online meeting.

Tips for successful online meetings
* Have an agenda, and stick to it.
* Circulate documents in advance, if possible.
* Set a time limit to help keep participants focused.
* Keep contributions succinct and to the point.
* Do not allow interruptions.

● Do not allow interruptions

8 Motivation and discipline

Motivating the team

Success as a team can often be all the motivation its members need to try their hardest. But don't rely on it alone. To keep the team functioning well, you may need to get out the carrots!

* **Reward** the whole team for success.
* **Reward** some individual work.
* **Encourage** the team members to recognize each other's contributions.

Alternatively, you may need the stick.

* **Crack down** on those who undermine the team.
* Guard against fragmentation.

Appreciation and rewards can work wonders

> **'You can motivate by fear. And you can motivate by reward. But both of these methods are only temporary. The only lasting thing is self-motivation.'**
>
> Homer Rice

While **discipline** is important, try to keep the work environment as informal as possible – people usually work better when they don't have their boss constantly looking over their shoulder. In addition, remember that, while **appreciation** and rewards can work wonders, the same incentives don't work on everyone.

● 'I thought if I brought in a carrot cake it might motivate the team!'

Rewards

Incentives can spur people in the right direction, but they have to be the right sorts of incentives. **Get to know your team** as individuals, so that you will understand what type of reward will motivate each one of them most effectively.

Team rewards

Most of the rewards should be for co-operation and team performance. **Celebrate** the team's successes at suitable times of the year or when **key milestones** are reached in a project. The rewards might be:

* a shared bonus
* an outing or meal paid for by the organization
* an early finish (or a late start the next day)
* lunchtime drinks.

Most rewards should be for co-operation and team performance

Individual rewards

Giving rewards for individual achievement is one sure way to **undermine team spirit**. For example:

* if there's a bonus for highest individual sales in a sales team, people will compete for it and keep promising leads and successful sales strategies to themselves
* if there's no advantage to co-operation, you'll probably get better sales through competition – and you can put this book down now.

During the forming stage, giving individual **rewards for co-operation** can be helpful. These should not be substantial enough to provoke jealousy and they should involve the rest of the team. So, instead of saying privately, 'I'm giving this as a thank you…' use a team meeting to say:

'This is a thank you from all of us.'

You're a hero

A better way to reward co-operation might be to get the team members to reward each other's efforts.

The reward in this case is purely nominal – a small chocolate – because what is really being given is **recognition** that the person is a valued member of the team. Its nominal nature should make for a good-natured, jokey atmosphere, in which people give more freely. Follow the steps in the table opposite.

You might make this a regular feature of team meetings.

'A group becomes a team when each member is sure enough of himself and his contribution to praise the skill of the others.'

Norman S. Hidle

You'll need a box of Heroes®.

1 Open the box	Tell the team that the chocolates are for heroes – people who have done something beyond their normal duties and made life easier for another team member.
2 Start things off by giving a Hero to your chosen person	Say, 'You're my hero because you handled that difficult customer for me/sorted out my spreadsheet/came in ten minutes early to get things ready/…' or whatever.
3 Invite people to give one to their own heroes	They can give to more than one person or to no one but when they do give, they must say why.

Stop after five minutes or so.

What, no Heroes?
Quality Street® or Roses® will do just as well, but you'll have to find a different form of words at step 2. Perhaps '… for improving the Quality of my life…' or '… I have only a Rose to give you…' Bad puns are welcome here!

Team discipline

In theory, if you can get the team to **bond** properly, and they have a clear view of their goals, then all should be well. In practice, not everyone is a team player and, despite your best efforts, cannot be turned into one.

* The **slacker** breeds resentment among those who do work hard.
* The **griper** undermines morale with endless complaining.
* The **jealous** will work against those seen to be more valued.
* The **creative free spirit** doesn't think the rules apply to 'the talent'.

They need to accept that the same rules and codes of behaviour apply equally to all members of the team, and to know that breaches will not be tolerated.

'One bad apple spoils the barrel.'
Proverb

● The slacker will breed resentment

92

Dealing with a staffing problem

Assume that the person is not aware that their behaviour is a problem. **Act promptly**, pointing out to them what they are doing and its effect on other members. This is often all the action necessary.

If that doesn't work:

* make the change of behaviour a performance target, and set a strict, close deadline.

If that doesn't work:

* think whether you can use them elsewhere.

And if that doesn't work:

* start dismissal proceedings according to your organization's policies.

Appeals to employment tribunals are expensive, time wasting and stressful for all concerned, so if the need for dismissal looks likely, you must document every incident and your actions, and take advice from your HR department or a solicitor.

Are happy teams more productive?

A feature of high-performing teams is that their members tend to be happier at work than those in less successful teams. Does this mean that you can make your team more efficient by making them happier? If you offer flexi-hours, a good pension plan, an attractive working environment or even just free doughnuts and coffee – all of which should make them happier – will these **increase productivity**?

The answer is 'not necessarily'. The evidence is that productive people show a higher rate of job satisfaction, but that it is the productivity that makes them feel good, not the other way round.

Top tip
To make your team more productive, concentrate your efforts on ensuring that they have the resources they need to do the job properly.

Best friends

Friendship between members of a team is positive, but very close friendships can be a problem. **Sub-groups** will form within teams when people who are working most closely together bond more strongly. This is good, as long as it does not become exclusive.

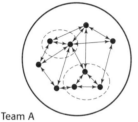

● Team A

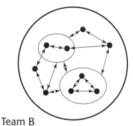

● Team B

* In team A the sub-groups are not exclusive, and there are bonds between a large number of the team members.

* Team B has two sub-groups and a few outsiders. For the outsiders, the only bond is to the sub-group, not to the people within it.

9 Bonding exercises

Building a united team

The members of a team should eventually bond together simply through doing whatever it is that the team does. However, anything you can do to kick-start and accelerate the **bonding process** will help produce a more united and more effective team, faster. The 'getting to know you' exercises and games in this chapter will help this process.

If people are new to each other, give everyone a badge showing their name and role.

A team should eventually bond simply through doing whatever it is that the team does

If your first meeting is round a table, prepare place markers along the same lines as the badges – a folded sheet of A4 will do the trick.

> **George Miller**
> Outreach Co-ordinator
>
> Call me: *Dusty*

● A name badge can be a good icebreaker

This chapter offers several exercises.

* **'Introductions'** and **'On a roll'** are icebreakers to enable team members to learn names and a little about each other.
* **'Who am I?'** will get people talking to each other.
* The two **'same but different'** games explore the diversities and similarities with a team.
* **'I did this well'** is for long-term use. Bonding exercises should not stop just because people know each other.

'Getting to know you' exercise

Introductions

Use this exercise with a new team if most of them are new to each other. If you are short of time, stop after step 3.

1 Ask people to turn to the person sitting to one side of them.
2 Give them two minutes to find out about each other.
3 Go round the group asking each person to introduce their partner.
4 Ask them to form into pairs again, but this time with the person on the other side.
5 Ask them to find out two new facts about each other.
6 Go round the group again, asking everyone to introduce their new partner and tell the group about them.

'Together Everyone Achieves More – an acronym for TEAM'

Anon.

The first round will normally bring out people's names, what they like to be called and something about their job, background or qualifications – but directly relevant to the group.

The second round should produce things like how they take their coffee, whether they are married, their hobbies, etc. – which may help to get the group to see each other more as people than as names and roles.

Having two rounds of introductions helps to fix more names to faces, and people will certainly remember the ones they have interviewed.

Make sure your teambuilding activities comply with equality and discrimination policy and law in respect of gender, race, disability, age, etc.

● Bonding with the team

'Getting to know you' games

Knowing names and roles is a start, but the team members need to start talking to each other so that they can begin to form relationships. Here are two informal **icebreaker** games.

On a roll

This could be played as an extension of or an alternative to the 'Introductions' icebreaker. There's a sting in the tail of this game – people who take more have to give more.

1 Pass a roll of toilet paper around the group, telling people to take as much as they like – but without telling them why.
2 Ask each person to share one fact about themselves for each square of toilet paper they are holding.

Team members need to start talking to each other

Who am I?

Here's another game that aims to break down barriers and make people feel more relaxed with one another. It could be played during a coffee break, when people need to be up and moving.

1 Write the names of famous people on Post-it® notes.
2 Stick one of the notes on the back of each team member.
3 People have to work out who they are by asking each other only yes/no questions.
4 The first person to find out who they are wins.
5 Continue until all (or most, if people are having trouble) find the answer.

Top tip
If your team members start talking freely, laughing and becoming energized, you know that your icebreaker has worked.

'Same but different' games

These two games are about the **things people have in common** – and that may not be apparent at first sight. It will help people see beyond the obvious and, by extension, encourage 'outside the box' thinking.

I'm different because...

This one can also be used as a 'getting to know you' exercise.

Each person must introduce themselves and say one way in which they are different from everyone else in the group. It can be a characteristic (not a visible one) or something they do or have done (not related to the job). If anyone else in the group can say 'Same here!' the speaker must try again.

● 'Has anyone else done this?'

104

We are the same because...

This exercise gets people to explore under the surface of their fellow team members. The more visibly diverse the group, the more useful you may find this.

1   Divide the group into sets of three or four.
2   Ask each set to find at least five things that every member has in common. People are not allowed to include obvious things or anything that all humans share.
3   After 15 minutes or so, ask each set to tell the rest of the group why they are the same.

'No member of a crew is praised for the rugged individuality of his rowing.'

Ralph Waldo Emerson

Valuing the team

I did this well

The purpose of this exercise is – superficially – for team members to tell others of their successes in their work. The deeper purpose is for people to receive **positive feedback** on their work so that members will feel valued by others in the team. It is also a useful exercise in **speaking and listening**.

1 Get people to form pairs.
2 In each pair, one person is to talk about one or more things that they have done well recently.
3 Their partner must listen without interruption or feedback, unless the talker starts to underplay what they have done. Then the listener should stop them by holding up a hand and say 'No'.
4 After three minutes, the partners change places and repeat the exercise.

What did we learn?

After the exercise, bring the group back together and discuss the following questions.

> *Was it easier to be the talker or the listener?*

> *How does it feel to sing your own praises, and to do this without feedback?*

> *Do you now see your contribution to the team in a different light?*

> *Is it hard to listen without interrupting?*

Variation

'I did this well' can be done as a **whole-group** exercise, but reduce the talking time if there are more than six or eight members, or the whole exercise could drag on. This approach gives the team leader a better chance to observe how the members rate themselves, and each other.

10 Exercises in communication and co-operation

Towards better teamworking

In this second selection of exercises, the emphasis is on developing the skills needed for **working together** more effectively. The exercises also show the value of good communication, by encouraging people to listen and talk to each other directly.

The activities also aim to improve co-operation. If a team sees that it can co-operate and solve problems together in one situation, it will carry that sense of success back into the work situation.

> **'If you can laugh together, you can work together.'**
> Robert Orben

If a team can solve problems in one situation, it will carry that sense of success back to its work

· ·

This chapter offers the following exercises.

* **'Are you listening?'** encourages better communication through active listening.
* **'Face value'** demonstrates how preconceptions can impede co-operation.
* **'It's a puzzle'** is a lesson in the value of co-operation within and between groups.
* **'The egg drop'** is a creative challenge and an opportunity to explore how roles develop within groups.

Are you listening?

Try this if you feel that some members of the team have communication problems. It will show how much they really listen to what others have to say, and help build listening skills.

You will need:

* a set of cards or pieces of paper, each with a controversial topic written on it, such as:
  » bank profits
  » euthanasia
  » faith schools
  » gay marriage
  » climate change theory
  » tax avoidance and benefits fraud.

You can duplicate topics but you must have at least six different ones, and you will need three times as many cards as participants.

● 'I'm not listening!'

The exercise

Explain the object and rules of the exercise carefully before you start.

1 Divide the group into pairs, giving each pair six different topic cards.
2 One in each pair takes a card and talks on the topic, without interruption, for three minutes.
3 The listening partner summarizes, in one minute, what the other has just said.
4 The speaker gives feedback on the accuracy of the summary.
5 Switch roles and repeat steps 2 to 4.
6 Bring the group back together and discuss what has been learned from the exercise about listening.

Variations

1 The listening partner summarizes the talker's views *to the group*. Knowing that the whole group will be judging the performance may spur people to greater efforts.
2 The listeners may ask questions if they don't understand a point.

Face value

The aim here is to show how the assumptions we make about people affect the way we interact with them, and how that can interfere with the smooth running of the team.

You will need:

* a label for each participant, written on Post-it® notes, which can be stuck directly on their forehead or on paper hats (if you've done the 'Who am I?' exercise in chapter 9).

The label can be descriptive, e.g. 'pushy', 'helpful', 'nice guy', 'untrustworthy', etc., or directive, e.g. 'agree with me', 'disagree with me', 'expect me to solve it', 'ignore me'.

● 'I'm sure this isn't me...'

114

The exercise

1 Divide the group into sets of five or six.
2 Hand out the labels, face down, one per person.
3 Ask each person to stick a label on their neighbour, without letting them see what is written on it.
4 Give each set a task, e.g. planning an outing. Each set could have a different task or they could all do the same thing.
5 People must treat each other according to their labels.
6 After five or six minutes, stop the exercise and let people read their labels.

What did we learn?

After the exercise, bring the group back together and discuss these questions:

* How far did each set get with the task?
* Did the labels interfere with it?
* How did people feel about the way they were treated?

It's a puzzle

This is an exercise in communication and **problem solving**, and a demonstration of the value of co-operation. It will get people talking within their group to solve the problem and establish roles, and between the groups to **negotiate**.

You need enough people to be able to split them into three or four groups, each of three (or possibly two) members.

You will need:

* one child's jigsaw of around 20 pieces for each group
* one plastic bag per group.

Before the exercise, break up each jigsaw, keeping back four pieces from each one if you have three groups and six pieces from each one if there are four groups. Place the remaining pieces of each jigsaw in a separate bag. Take the pieces you kept back and place two pieces from each of the different puzzles in each of the other bags.

The exercise

1 Divide the team into groups.
2 Hand a bag containing puzzle pieces to each group.
3 Give this instruction: 'Complete your puzzles as quickly as possible. There are no rules.'
4 Leave them to it and refuse to answer any questions.
5 Stop when all the puzzles have been completed or a stalemate is reached.

What did we learn?

Once people realize that the bags contain mixed pieces, they have to work out ways of getting their missing pieces from the other groups. If groups **compete**, negotiations can get complex and take time. If they **co-operate**, all the puzzles can be completed quickly.

'We must all hang together, or assuredly, we shall all hang separately.'

Benjamin Franklin

The egg drop

Allow around 90 minutes for this exercise in teamwork, where **ingenuity** and **creativity** count. The aim is to build a package for a single egg that would protect that egg in a fall from the top shelf in the supermarket – about 2 m (6 ft). The team must also produce a brief jingle or sales pitch for the package.

For each group you will need:

* 1 egg, uncooked
* 6 drinking straws
* 1 reel of sticky tape
* 1 sheet packaging cardboard/1 thick envelope/2 paper towels (optional).

● 'Mmm…could be messy.'

118

The exercise

1 Divide the team into groups of four or five.
2 Hand out the materials and explain the challenge.
3 Allow 30 minutes to create the packaging and sales pitch/jingle.
4 Gather together and listen to each sales pitch. Take a vote to decide the best.
5 Take the results outside to test them.
6 Hand out the prizes (a creme egg each) to the group whose egg sustains least damage.

What did we learn?

✳ How were tasks allotted in each group?
✳ Did a leader emerge?
✳ Was everyone meaningfully engaged?
✳ How were design decisions made?

(Courtesy of Wilderdom)

What next?

You may find these books and websites useful:

Cole Miller, Brian, *Quick Team-Building Activities for Busy Managers* (New York: AMACOM, 2004)

McKee, Scot, *Creative B2B Branding (no really)* (Oxford: Goodfellow Publishers, 2010)

Robbins, Stephen, *The Truth about Managing People* (Harlow: Pearson Education, 2008)

www.actiondays.com (corporate event organizers)

www.businessballs.com (ideas)

www.freshtracks.co.uk (ideas, team activities and conference organizers)

www.wilderdom.com (ideas and materials)